MOVING TARGETS

MOVING TARGETS

JEN WEBB

RECENT
WORK
PRESS

Moving Targets
Recent Work Press
Canberra, Australia

Copyright © Jen Webb, 2018

ISBN: 9780648257981 (paperback)

 A catalogue record for this book is available from the National Library of Australia

All rights reserved. This book is copyright. Except for private study, research, criticism or reviews as permitted under the Copyright Act, no part of this book may be reproduced, stored in a retrieval system, or transmitted in any form by any means without prior written permission. Enquiries should be addressed to the publisher.

Cover photograph: 'Cementerio bajo cero' by Inko 6 reproduced under Creative Commons Attribution licence 2.0
Cover design: Recent Work Press
Set by Recent Work Press

recentworkpress.com

Dedicated to Karen Mow, with admiration

Contents

Section 1: Building the family tree

After the carnival	
I	1
II	2
III	3
The good eye	
I	4
II	5
III	6
IV	7
Blanche and Henry	
I	8
II	9
III	10
IV	11
The end of the affair	12
At the Unsicht-Bar, Berlin	13
Narcolepsy	
On the plane	14
On the train	15
Stasis	16
Boatbuilding in the Coromandel	
1980	17
1985	18
1990	19
1995	20
The Long Man of Wilmington	21
Waiting for the phone to ring	22
The judge	23
Fairy tales	24

In the garden
    Spring   25
    Summer   26
    Autumn   27
    Winter   28
No time like the present   29
Dinner party   30
After the flood   31
Parkrun   32
At the Repat Hospital, Heidelberg
    The night watch   33
    The morning shift   34
    Afternoon   35
    Outpatient   36
    Later   37
    Later still   38

Section 2: Mythologies

The loom   41
Metamorphosis
    I   42
    II   43
    III   44
Icarus
    I   45
    II   46
    III   47
    IV   48
    V   49
Sibyl
    I   50
    II   51
    III   52
    IV   53

V	54
VI	55
VII	56
Medusa	57
Ariadne	58
Into exile	
Aeneas escaping Troy	59
Aeneas deserting Dido	60
Aeneas finding Rome	61

Section 3: The Principles of War

Third degree	
I	65
II	66
III	67
On the highveld	68
First responders, 1944	69
House arrest	70
Preparations for the siege	71
Moving targets	
I	72
II	73
III	74
After the disaster	75
War zone	
I	76
II	77
III	78
IV	79
On the picket line	80
Afterword	83

Section 1: Building the family tree

'I told her I'd had seven lovers, but I'd like you to know that isn't true'
(the Lunar Woman, talking to Simone de Beauvoir, from *Letters to Sartre*)

After the carnival

(after Anne Carson)

I

Bittersweet. The honey on my tongue. The scent of flowers when they're on the turn. You touched me, after all these years, and in that touch was our history, sweet passion, bitter end. A hail of soft consonants and cracked vowels and you, my longing and my love, stitched into one poor self.

II

We play that drinking game. Never have I ever—stolen gloves on a winter day. Never have I ever treated my marriage vows like confetti. Never have I ever: forgotten to pay the bill; rejected the dog when he was seeking assurance; eaten your last cookie though you'd begged me to leave it for tomorrow. I wake in the mornings wracked with shame, hunting for my phone keys glasses purse. The cat raps at the door, and I do what I'm told. Never have I ever loved you, fucked you, broken every vow for you. Never have I ever let you know.

III

Most love ends badly. If we had stayed where we first found ourselves: stoned behind the shower block in the caravan park; on the long distance bus where you had commandeered my seat; in the line at the organic vegetable store; at the conference dinner where you caught my eye and I could have fucked you right there and then. When it became later, but not yet too late, we found ourselves in the apartment high above Granville Street with—if you stood on tiptoe—a view of the sea. How sweet you tasted then: every breath straight out of Sappho. If we had stayed there, and avoided all that was to come. How sweet our love. How bitter.

The good eye

I

Brush the petals from your hair: a high wind is blowing and the air is all blossom. You are gazing out across the orchard, your eyes full of tomorrow. If I touch you will you turn, or return? I tune the guitar and begin playing, very softly, one of those old arpeggios you use to sing yourself to sleep. The music slides around you, each broken chord leaning forward and then curling back, spiralled like petals on a stem, and despite yourself you start to sing.

II

You are painting again. Charge your brush and lay out a line, a cyan that shimmers and is gone. You step back, and look intently at the canvas, then load up a dense vermilion, and place it in just the right spot. Stand back again, use the palette knife to correct an edge. Your oils are water, your canvas merely the sky. When it dries you will varnish the work, sealing in colours that only you can see.

III

Today you use a roller, dipped deep. Spatter never bothers me: the world becomes pointillist once the painting's done. Today the walls are hard grey clashed against yellow —my choice, though it gives me vertigo—and the floors are spilt white milk. When I fall you kneel beside me, and gently spoon fugitive blue all over my limbs.

IV

Squeeze the paint from the tube: the palette bursts into red. The world is fading to sepia, you say, and only we can return it to light. Your stained hand, your presumptive eye. Spin the colour wheel: cobalt or magenta, vermilion or teal? When the wheel stops you squeeze more paint, and stir. How little it takes to make a change: only an eye for colour, a surface to paint, a hand to guide the flow.

Blanche and Henry

I

He gives me words, when all I asked for was line. He brushes me off, draws me close. Makes me see how light floods the paper and then dark floods the paper and how faces and trees and hands take shape across the white. Makes me see how the alchemy of fluid and light draws us together and apart, how it fills every space. But I was talking about line, I say, not light. Hush, says Henry, and he talks on, shifting photos from tray to line, and words pile up around me, a wall.

II

She sang out a goodbye, stepped into the cab, pulled down the seat. *Go, go.* Her face averted. She found paper and pencil, swiped at the tears, began to write. Standing still in the darkroom, Henry flicks on the lights, and reaches for the mop. The hypo is all over the floor. The settling trays upended. At least the films are safe. Chemicals fizz at the back of his throat. Henry covers his eyes with his hands. Wonders if he looks different, smudged, washed out. She has fogged him, the way a touch of light will fog a film.

III

Inside the book he has sent her she finds a photograph. It is her, of course, in black and white. Early sun pours in past the curtains he drew back to light her. It is her, sitting in his bed, holding his sheet to her heart, and there, on the back of her hand, that burn from where the hypo splashed. The smudge on her hand, her tangled morning hair, her breast. Mirrored in her eyes a shape that might be him. The burn has never healed. She treasures it, the mark on her skin, the proof that he was there.

IV

Five years ago I could have loved you, perhaps. Now there are weddings and babies and homes between us, and what might have been is just a shadow on the plate. You stood beside me in the dark; chemicals on your skin; the safe-light red on your cheek. I could have kissed you right then, but. The image is burning on the sheet, the hypo-wash has splashed across the floor. When I reach for you I hear, through the felted doors, the sound of passing bells. They are playing my song. Face it, Blanche. We are always in the dark.

The end of the affair

Evening is falling all over the city, and the tower is gathering grey around its shoulders, readying for sleep. Down in the Campbelltown train the travellers have settled in, shoulder to shoulder, on seats and in the aisles, rocking as one around the bends. You reach for me, privately, though there's no privacy here. Every bone aches for you, but it's the wrong place, the wrong time. We are on the downward slope, darling. It was good while it lasted. Keep saying that: *it was good while it lasted*; and we played our parts exceptionally well. I know you want to talk it out but I have locks to change, accounts to close, crockery to smash. I'll call you later. When the tree remembers to make new leaf; when the bees find their way back to the yard; when the broken magpie finds its voice: I promise I'll call.

At the Unsicht-Bar, Berlin

When he led us through the doorway we met what we had been told to expect: nothing. I could hear you across the table setting, could hear those near—or far, who can tell?—in the limitless black. That's all I know. In the dark, blind waiters chirped and clicked. You poured champagne on the tablecloth. I forked truffle-scented pasta at my chin. When you fell silent I reached out a hand and encountered a slice of the world. I'm not a proud woman, but what I did there makes me blush, even now. Later you said it wasn't you, but who among us really knows who we are in the dark?

Narcolepsy

On the plane

Light is seeping through the cloud, snow courses like veins across the tops of hills, we are beginning our descent and all large electronic devices must be put away. Below the snow are burnt-toast fields, neglected, crop circled. This is the wrong country for that sort of carry-on. I shoot a photograph but all it shows is blur. In the seat beside me you twitch in your sleep and call out someone else's name. Or perhaps you are feigning sleep. It's hard to tell.

On the train

Passengers are sitting or standing or crabbing between luggage and legs. You critique my style; the shameful tears rise and I blink them away, blaming allergy. We pass small towns, small houses, each with an elbow-wide garden, a tiny shed and a shrub. Small towns with allotments picked out between the fences, and in one a man in overalls, tying up his tomatoes. The train is running late: you keep sighing, irritatedly, or falling asleep.

Stasis

It's not yet day, not by a long shot, but intimations of light beckon through the blinds. You shift yourself in our crisp cool bed, slide back into sleep. Dream-stuff shifts below your lids, your hands open, slowly, and then close. This is when I like you best: far from thought, close to hand. Sleep on, while you can. The day is readying itself.

Boatbuilding in the Coromandel

(for AB)

1980

We walked together down through the naked winter trees to the creek, weaving between ancient trees, picking out the narrow path in the deep grey of morning. Breathe deeply, darling: this is ancient air. Skippers and orb weavers, hummers and singers and whistlers accompany our steps. They call out as I reach for you, and ducking through the tui's liquid call we slip and skid through mud, down the steep track. When I fell you helped me up, when you stumbled I gave you my hand. Then it was the edge of the river, grey stones and bronze, sheer water. You stripped off, you stripped me off, we stepped into the river. Trembling, a foal on new legs, an invalid finding his feet. You stretch out your hands, fingers splayed, feeling for what is solid. Trembling, I lean into the current, I slip a hand into yours, you turn to me fish-mouthed. Holding tightly to each other, our feet feeling their uncertain way, your skin speaks to mine.

1985

Two days of rain and the creeks are full and rushing. We step cautiously from stone to stone, crossing the water, and the current tugs at our feet. Playing possum, you call it, and I decide not to tell you that you've got it wrong. Later we are driving down the Thames; falling rocks block the road and we wait, a link in a chain, for someone to clear the way.

I am running out of things to say. I try this gambit and that but they trail off mid phrase. You pat my hand, absently, touching me the way you do: quick and capable, and then nothing. You tilt the rear vision mirror toward you, the side mirror, check this side and that. Which smile is best? you ask, and I shrug, watching you watch yourself, absorbed. The afternoon light casts petals on your cheek, shades the stories in your eyes.

If I leave the car, will you know? I close the door quietly, and lean against the hill. You make a gesture I can't read, and then the sun cascades through the storm front, scattering rainbows, and the bellbirds fly up, delighted, singing up the storm.

1990

You had laid the pohutakawa knees in the brackish stream and let them marinade for months. You had built your Heath Robinson steamer, and fired it, and cooked the planks til they cried uncle and bent themselves into unfamiliar lines. Then it was copper screws, and rabbit glue, and clamps, and then the knees, dried and baked, that you tapped between the seams. While the ship took shape between your hands I wove hammocks, and stitched the sail, and coiled perfect ropes. When it was done, you said, we'd head to the islands and live on taro and beer. When it was done we christened it, in the orthodox way. You touched me hard, there on the weather deck, me crying uncle, but then you noticed the mast tilted, and the tiller not true, and you turned back to your blueprints.

1995

Those things we can neither forget nor forgive: like Chappell bowling underarm, like the day you caught me out and burned my clothes and tore up my books. Things we have almost forgotten: like that day at the wharf where I threw you a line and you failed to catch it; like that day I scrabbled through the ballast looking for anything I could discard.

We have been years together, more than anyone expected. The plans you sowed, and scattered, and shredded. You can't remember now what we did, or why. Don't you recall that night you went up en pointe, reached out, and and found star dust on your fingers? You smeared it all over me, laughing.

How could you bear to let me leave? Give me your hand; remember how it felt to hold me.

The Long Man of Wilmington

You drove me along narrow roads between hedgerows to see the ancient horse, picked out in chalk, on a green hillside. We walked to meet it, ankle deep in the soil. That's the aroma of antiquity, you said, though I hadn't asked. Centuries of people pacing the field, watching daffodils blossom and willows grow and then die. I reached for you, with your grey English skies, your green fields. The centaur in you meeting the druid in me. Don't we make a pair?

Waiting for the phone to ring

The fields are grey, reflecting the sky, but once the sun is high they will be green again. He can see the thread of fence where faint sparks show the wires have slipped off their insulators. He curses the young steers who push against the metal fence posts, testing their nerve against the shock. Boys will be boys. He whistles up the dogs, hunts out his boots. Behind him the phone rings, but it won't be her, not this early. He shuts the kitchen door.

The judge*

(for RG)

He knows he is a cliché: a man in a horsehair wig. He loves the way he looks, though he'd never confess it. Any opportunity to step out of the courthouse and stride along George Street to the coffee shop, turning heads. He *carpe diem*s. He lives alone. No, he lives with a patient partner, who has his or her own career and concerns. They make a point of eating out together at least once a week. Turning heads. He lives with a cat, who is aging and needs dental care. No, it's a dog, a setter who needs daily exercise. He pays a young woman to feed and walk the dog, and to tidy the house. He leaves cash for her, on the kitchen counter. The camera hidden above the bookshelf records all she does, and at night he plays back the recording, wearing his wig, his robe, nothing else.

---

*"Now and then a lewd picture will catch the eye of a judge". From 'URGENT NOTICE for every Police Officer', Ross Gibson, May 2015

Fairy tales

I am the ugly sister, cutting off my toes to spite my feet, and now that I've lost all sense of balance I walk as naked people do—fast and awkward, on the balls of my feet. No doubt there were other choices I could have made along the way, accommodations I could have selected, but we all work with what we've got. Me, with mutilated feet and furious mind. You, with your hummingbird heart. We limp on, by some accounts a match.

In the garden

Spring

The basil went in first. Tomatoes were straightforward, though we had words about the marigolds. You turn the soil, and it crumbles, reeking of compost, of blood and bone. We slip cucumbers into their spot, and aubergines. I am visualising produce I will never harvest, food I will never prepare. The sun is soft on the back of my neck, bees wait for flowers and worms for new water. Later, the scent of leaves will fill the back yard and the green plants nod in early evening sun.

Summer

First we cut down the big gum, but it was rotting from the inside out, and what with Arthur next door being taken out by a widow-maker we didn't want the risk. Next we cut down the cherry tree because it wasn't thriving. The boronia died by its own hand. We cut down the photinia because its foetid stench filled our room on summer mornings. The grevillea died, and the callistemon, and the kunzea. Now the finches flutter above our heads, begging for trees. Now the honeyeaters complain, fiercely.

Autumn

Cracks in the concrete. Contrails betraying the sky. A cold breeze has arrived and petals are falling from the quince. The arborist lays his hands on E Bansksii, closes his eyes, then leans in for a closer look. She's a good one, he pronounces. Got years in her yet.

Winter

You sourced the stones and the stone mason. You stood, watching, while the workmen cut and troweled and tapped and shaped. All you wanted was a wall where you could plant mesembryanthemums and small tough ferns, and stand in the evening sun, gin softening in the glass, and picture a wall of colour, a tomorrow when everything would be true, a future where no one, not ever, never again, would die.

No time like the present

I picture my father walking the Country Club greens: he has hit his ball into the sand trap and he makes his stroke, a whirlpool of sand. I imagine his pratfall death, his friends reaching out too late as he falls, still laughing. Now he is elsewhere, despite his panicked friends, despite his favourite clubs, despite the family who do not want to take that call.

I picture my uncle who quarrelled with time, and who removed the hands from all his clocks then hung them ticking blindly on the walls. They are failing there still, still trying to sound the hour.

I picture my son picking through folders for the one document that will prove the point. He is on the last stretch; he has stapled history to the wall; he opens the archive, and selects a file.

Dinner party

We cooked beetroot and beans, we sliced bread and spread hummus. I gave you promises I didn't mean to keep. You gave me a handful of hope. Together we shelled the hard boiled eggs, and grilled asparagus and cheese. As the sun drifted across the day, as people came and went, staying long enough to drink our whisky and eat the muffins, we seized moments for thought. By midnight the day was wrung out, the cats were making their way back home and the neighbours had gone to bed. You reached for me and said 'let's call it good'.

After the flood

Mostly it's cleaning up, the working party arriving with hoes and leather gloves, all day picking and cutting and burning, so people like us can cycle unobstructed through the park.

Mostly it's covering the field, sealing the holes through which god knows what can squeeze—something from a small child's nightmare that slithers against your knees. My own nightmares are the tedium of paperwork. A credit not entered. A lost receipt lost. Mostly about leaving things that matter on public transport, not getting to the terminal on time.

Don't go too soon, dearest. I haven't heard your dreams.

Parkrun

Winter, and early sun has licked the frost from a corner of the park bench. She sits there, poised, breathing. If ice still addresses her skin, she does not know; she will not know. It is not a morning for being cold. It is a morning for starting again.

Breathing done, she unwinds herself from the spool of the day, stands, and starts to run. Keeping fit whatever the weather. You're not well, he says, but he cycles alongside, keeping watch. Over her frail body, unshriven but innocent under his hands, under the hands of that stranger who stepped unbidden from the back of the bar. Remembering that: *Do you have no pity?* he asks, peddling hard to keep up, *no regrets?* No, she says. None.

At the Repat Hospital, Heidelberg

(for H)

The night watch

In the corridor nurses are singing along to the radio. The old man by the window coughs; slips back into snoring; coughs.

Strange silence. You can hear a spider preparing her new web in a corner where no one cleans. And ghosting in, the crackle of light glancing off crosses in the memorial garden, in the *lest we forget* we have all forgotten.

You, by the door, listening to the night, to its three-part harmony: the lilt of voices; the murmur of skin as it shifts across bones; the drip of fluids.

This is the time the curtains are drawn, sheets bundled from the room, the bodies removed. This is when the demobbed return, those we see only when the light falls just so. They walk through these old halls, touching new instruments with astounded hands.

The room is dark, but if you step out boldly, small lights stutter up to illuminate deadfalls and pits. There will be better news; you can count on it; and this time our hearts will unbreak.

The morning shift

There are trolleys in the hall. You hear the cracking of cups, a dropped spoon. A light bulb plays the string sections of the score and your fingers move against the bedspread, tapping out the scherzo of the ward. Muted; still irrepressible.

Padding of soft-shod feet on tiled floors. The awkward chiming of the succour bells. You lie back on the hospital bed, blood draining slowly from your wounds.

Outside, a flag drifts in the afternoon breeze. Inside the nurses come and go, chatting, while you sink into morphine; while outside someone is driving down Bell Street passing six streets all named High; while someone somewhere is dying but it is not you.

Afternoon

The nurses know what we wish we didn't know: how quickly hours are consumed, how the days run out, how time fades through sepia to black.

Every call is urgent. People in blue keep passing your door, pushing trolleys, pushing wheeled chairs. A tritone bell sounds, announcing an emergency in unit 3, and men in white stroll to the crisis. A code blue in neurology. Another catastrophe in another ward. We sit together, holding hands for courage, here where the body fails, where lines of flight end only at the wall. We sit together, waiting, here where there is no easy way out.

Later you wait, alone. Something presses against your spine but you can't remember what happened yesterday or the day before. Strangers comment on your blood pressure, your heart. Strangers comment on how you will not manage, not given the harm. You could weep, but if once you start there'll be no going back.

Outpatient

What we did today was wash the floor, and wash the kitchen counters, and take endone, and turn foodstuffs into food, and take endone, and walk the dog, and take the tot to the playground, and take endone, and make phone calls, and find that lost form. What we did today was avoid the open wounds, and avoid the thought of tomorrow, and avoid reading the news.

Later

We slice the ginger and shallots. Dredge the tofu. Chop coriander and string the snow peas. I toast cashews while you julienne the chili and set the rice to boil. The house is full of scent: sesame and soy. This is new food: it will repair broken flesh. The baby has had his bath, and you have poured the wine. Outside the sun is going down and the late wind breathes clean air in through the kitchen window.

As long as we remember, as long as we refuse to forget, as long as the tests keep coming up trumps. We will keep making plans. We will not give way.

A small child runs to you, arms extended, and you swing him to the ceiling. Off stage a dog barks, high pitched and joyful. A toddler balances at the top of the stairs, a child swings on the door. The future is here with us, running full tilt through every room and its rush into the now leaves us gasping.

Later still

You walk through the hospital and pause, hearing the mutter of anticipated memory, voices of babies still to be born, of people assuming death. You shrug your bag onto your shoulder and find the door. Between last year's crisis and all the crises to come, the ones still lacing their boots and looking for their keys, you keep walking.

Section 2: Mythologies

'Poetry, since it defies scientific analysis, must be rooted in some sort of magic, and that magic is disreputable.'
Robert Graves, *The White Goddess*

The loom

She has hauled out her loom, though she'd sworn she'd never touch it again. But he brought her those skeins of mohair and silk, crimson and garnet and rose. She hauls out her loom, warps it up with torn linen and old photos and the ghosts of letters she never sent. Then it's the rush of shuttle, the clack of shed stick, the slow magic as images turn into form. He comes to the studio sometimes, but he cannot make sense of what she is making. She has written it in a language he does not know, a language of being left alone and then reclaimed; of fists against walls and nights without rest; of the body, and of blood.

Metamorphosis

I

The strangeness between parent and child, now adult to adult, almost matched. Still she can reduce you with a gesture, with a phrase. Reminders of you before it was you. Reminders that once you were completely loved, that once you sang yourself into language, while she sang back to you; that once you conducted the world with small inquisitive hands. You stand taller, forget the toddler self who in a guilty corner is still trying to work it all out.

II

She stands beside the window and turns her hand, contemplating its shape. The knuckles are more than they were, the skin less. It has changed colour, changed form. Little by little she is becoming tree. Turns quickly to catch herself unaware in the mirror. Not quick enough. Now he is beside her, has come in on cat's feet. *Pick a card*, he says, and offers a choice of two. *It's nothing, or crone.* She chooses crone.

III

Like a fledgling who hasn't yet figured out what wings mean, you run, each pace a fragment of flight. You are racing against the clock, and each interruption adds seconds and minutes to your time. Crossing the road. Pausing because a bird. The lace on your left shoe keeps coming undone, and the finish line is still so far ahead. Fly, if you can. Spread your lovely wings, cast yourself upon the currents of air, and fly.

Icarus

I

The hollow inside; the dark on her skin; the high thin cries of children or cats or birds, drifting. No one is coming to help. No one remembers her name. She is poised on the rocks, feathers on her shoulders, goose fat on her arms. It's cold up there: time to get going. Stretch your arms. She is flying, on ill-built wings, and close to the cliff she sees the warning sign. A hundred metres below, a partridge cries. Don't look down: you can't help here. She beats her wings. Tries to get some lift. Tries to craft some air.

II

How we flew, strapped into harness, ducking as missiles creased the air around our heads. We careened down the snakes, scrambled up ladders. When I slipped you saved me. When you flagged I cheered you on. Everyone said about you and me that … no, it's gone. There's just a spatter of dust where the memory was. There's just a welt raised on my skin, a dressing removed without ceremony.

III

He was a lot closer to the ground than he'd planned. The prison walls were lower than he'd calculated, his jerry-built wings had less lift than the maths had implied. He flew across the island, flapping like a hummingbird, frantic to get to deep water before he ran out of shallow air.

IV

They cut your wings, appalled, when the buds burst through your skin. You said you didn't mind. Wings hurt, the air offers no escape. I smeared arnica across the wounds, massaged oil across your back. You held me, fucked me, told me it felt like flying.

V

He has been flying too long. Minutes, months, hours; he's lost track. His back hurts, and his eyes, burnt by the sun. Nothing looks right from above. Fish eye lenses suspended from each overpass, the threat of billboards. If he'd ignored his father. If he could go back to being who he was, that shining child. Now it's dullness, and the beating of wings, and too hot flooded by too cold. No going back, no triumphal landing on the edge of the shore and calling out, *not dead yet!*

Sibyl

I

Lay out the cards. Play the Wise Child. The world has come to her just as she had planned. She is on a journey, but this is no pilgrimage, no quest. All she need do is move from space to space. Step between questions. Design her own maps.

II

She sits upright in the seat, eyes to the screen. 'This is your captain speaking'. Her hands are quiet but she pretends she is knitting: the tug of wool against skin, the click of needles; it calms her, passes the time. She imagines you at the door, coming to set her free, she imagines standing up and stepping away, stretching, and walking to the door. As though any options could be hers.

III

Meals the size of mice, water in cracked jars. Nothing tastes like anything he knows, he can't remember seeing any sun, is beginning to think he's never seen a tree. Chewing his ragged nails, breathing in the ice, he thinks how it is when the snow comes, and the squirrels menace. The only way out is out.

IV

Twenty thousand feet up, and still rising. Outside is dark, but those distant lights imply roads, and homes, and small towns. There is no one here but me, and a lot of space, and a woman offering me drinks. The lights drift gently, unmoored. Listen to the silence of all those who have gone into the city and closed their doors. I think about you often, how could I not, but all I hear is absence, and shredded notes.

V

I am not facing in the right direction. I am not sitting in my allocated seat. Uniformed men pace the aisle, making judgments. I am not confident that I can pass their tests. It's not that I'm disingenuous: all my history is of being found out. But I am not the one you were looking for. When I close my eyes, I see black. When I close my ears, the faintest thrum of your last song cuts through. I am not, all the same, coming home.

VI

You are cursing, there in the pilot's seat, controls sluggish as syrup and you without the manual. You push buttons, turn knobs, flick switches off and on. We should not be here. Phones can't connect, the engine coughs like a ram, a door begins to flap. When a murmur of starlings spirals past, swooping and falling, the plane drops in behind them, eager to impress. It tries out some steps, clumsy as a clog-dance, missing every mark. *We are out of place*, I say out loud. *We are out of grace*. And you shoot me a look, intimate as a blow.

VII

It doesn't get any realer than this: propelled cheek by jowl through the underworld, a game of sardines played with strangers. The kid pressed up against me is sleeping on his feet, breathing fumes against my neck. The woman pressed up against me is weeping. This, she says, is not where she had planned to be. Everyone is melting. A child cries out once, then falls into silence. Even our dreams have fractured, a gap opening between who we are and who we wish we were. There is no light at the end of this tunnel.

Medusa

I am ready for the night. There's a dab of scent between my breasts, a hyacinth planted in my ear, toads at my feet, and my thighs are clad in toitoi straps. A weta is perched on my forehead, a dugite slung about my neck. You tell me all this is metaphor, but I've seen you catch flies to feed the toads, and mice for the snakes, I've watched you cut the hyacinths and arrange them in jam jars, and everywhere I walk there's the scent of summer.

Ariadne

You want to make me come?—then come as you are: as god, not bull or swan. No more tired tricks. I wait for you, knee deep in the waters of Naxos. I wait for you, the thread around my own throat, singing myself against the stars. I am waiting.

Into exile

Aeneas escaping Troy

The plane is loading fast, passengers stowing their bags and taking their seats, and the cockpit door is open. He can see down the aisle and through the window to where lights break on the runway and, further away, the fire and the reason they are moving fast, travelling light, preparing for flight. The captain turns to eye up his passengers, and the crew members go through the motions. Then they are airborne, looking through the portholes at what they have just escaped, walls of fire, and behind that, black.

Aeneas deserting Dido

The way she walks ahead of him, her buttocks swelling and flattening with each step. His hands know their muscle, and the turn to softness when she straddles him —the thought of it still shakes him, even after all these months. *She is so*—he scratches for the right word, he has forgotten so much since going into exile, though 'exile', that's a word that for ten years and more has been on the tip of his tongue—*so capable*, he thinks. His Dido. Always on top of her game. He trails behind, watching the movement of her hips, choreographing tonight's encounter, knowing that this can't last, won't last, that he has something burnt about him, something that won't heal, that the fire is following him. He cannot stay.

Aeneas finding Rome

He called it 'finding' though it had never been mislaid. But when he lifted his ancient father from the boat, and lifted his small son from the boat, and stood with them between the sea and the unfamiliar hills, he realised that he at least had been found. He gathered wood, and set a fire: this was no time for niceties. What happened next has been expunged from the story. The blood, the burning. But it's over now, and he is here, still bearing the dead weight of all he left behind, still waking at night in breathless panic. They are all there, Aeneas and his father and his son, alive again each morning, forgetting Troy and the journey and what they did to claim this land, forgetting their lost lives, the bones they could not gather, the graves they never filled.

Section 3: The Principles of War

'War is no pastime; no mere passion for venturing and winning; no work of a free enthusiasm'.
Carl von Clausewitz, *On War*

Third degree

I

First we knew of it was the hammering on the door. When the upstairs-room guy drew back the bolts a rush entered, the sound of dogs howling, and the stained glass panel fell from its lead and lay in bright patches on the floor between spills of light. *Patterns of eternity*, someone murmured and the rest said *hush*. Clearly someone had done something wrong, but no one was about to confess. They led us to the van, chained in a line like circus elephants. We filed out, heads lowered, swaying from side to side.

II

So you make your way as instructed to where the soldiers are. Possibility of making good. You stand as instructed by the window on the seventh floor. Through the glass the sun sets, lighting up the lake. He says it's all being recorded, but you don't like to ask. Take a seat as instructed and spend the next hour with the generals. *It's their job*, he murmurs, close to your ear: *don't take it personally.* Yes you're afraid but you've been trained. Show no emotion: let the dark flow in.

III

This is no place for memory. Forget the way the sudden wind lifted and then dropped you, the water that swept the road and is rushing now over fractured stones. Forget the swirl and steel and poisoned air as the vehicles pass, sirens singing. At each intersection the red man follows the green man too soon and you have lost your way. What are you doing here, where rivers break faith, where macaques in the playground and seagulls in the park cry out for attention? Run, while you can.

On the highveld

The air is thin, sunbleached, a day-time white-sky that at twilight turns to fire. Then it's night, and the *son et lumière* of searchlights and storms. We sit in the back garden, beside the pool, drinking wine. The air smells of money, the water of cyanide and tears. We are breathless, we are burning, we are doing fine. Early morning and early evening, past the long tired queues at the bus stops, you drive me into town and we listen, trapped in traffic, to the singing of strangers caged in cars, singing in five-part harmony, a small gesture, a spell against what waits.

First responders, 1944

(for Mary)

When the missiles arrived, firemen were always first on the scene, and then the baker, his van now named hearse. Old men and young appeared, to haul the dead and damaged from the ruins. Brace yourself, they told each other. She drove a car that now was named ambulance. It was difficult to navigate the streets, she tells me, what with the rubble, the wounded moaning in their seats, the bodies and parts of bodies.

It's the eyes that get to you, she says. Their arms and legs are curved like infants', but their hearts are not. Scoop them up anyway. One or other will sometimes soften against you: a ripple of muscle under skin, almost a touch. But it only lasts a moment.

Don't look them in the eye.

By the fifth time someone passed her a paper bag containing hand or foot or head, she had learned not to shriek. By the fifth week she had learned not to see.

House arrest

It wasn't the worst of it, not by a long shot, but the falling angel took us by surprise, as did the wombat we found banging on the back door. The worst was when they took away the men and boys, when they shot the dogs. Each morning I chant affirmations, staring into the mirror I cracked six years ago and eight months. There's just four months more of bad luck. Possums scratch at the window, magpies call at the door. I will bury the dogs, visit the police station each day, hang your hat in its place above our bed. I will wait for these months to pass.

Preparations for the siege

How the train trembles, running through the suburb where matching houses stare blank-eyed toward the track and I gaze back, blank. Beyond the suburbs there's grassy fields, green abutting blue, and the sky leans down to lay its cheek against the hill. My ears ache, and my thighs, and the bruises on my breasts and arms. What doesn't kill me, et cetera. Now I'm gone, clackety clack, beyond the sadness of suburbs, into what I don't yet know, and I lay my face against the window, white on white, trembling.

Moving targets

I

When the moment came we gathered our bedding and silverware. We locked the house.

The road was neither long nor short. It merely was. One foot, then the other, such a long way to go, a step and a step and then another step.

Best times were when we walked, one foot then another. Worst times were lying in the ditch, arms like shields above our heads. I pissed myself of course, but after it happened three four five times I lost all shame.

We left so long ago. The road unscrolls before us, and we keep walking, and every moment looks the same, and every moment tastes like something I have never known. When the rain comes we curl in on ourselves, backs to the weather, gut and faces dry. Our bags are heavy, and our legs, our hearts. We keep climbing. There is nowhere left to go, but we have not yet arrived.

II

We sailed under nineteen bridges and walked across the three the boat couldn't squeeze below, not with us standing there straining at the oars. We carried the boat, though it weighed too much and the bridges complained and we held our breath and trod lightly to ease the load. We could have borrowed transport, said the locals, but the horse they offered favoured one foot, and its coat stared back at us, and we thought it wiser, all things considered, to make our own way. *Maybe there's a better way* we asked each other at nights, sitting around the only fires we could coax from that land, spilling water from cupped hands, spitting out teeth. Maybe there's a better way?

III

It's never just the bombs or the guns. It's never just the earthquakes or floods. It's the sharp edge of morning, the astringent taste of the Swiss bank. It's history that wakes up each day with a hangover, and then groans, complains about the light, begs for coffee. I pull the covers up to its chin, leave aspirin on the bedside table, switch off the lamp. This is nobody's land, nobody's truth. The dead are too many to count; the living keep swelling the coffers; we have gone too far to turn back.

After the disaster

All along the railway line houses are opening their doors and spilling dogs and children and toys across what is left of their lawns. Photographers lean from train windows, prowl up and down streets, searching for their Dorothea Lange moment. Each of us plans to be the one who records the passage of air across a dying land, who preserves the fragments that remain. The camera's eye is cold but accurate. We trawl the city and the suburbs, *semper paratus*, making history.

War zone

I

It is two a.m. and I am walking to and fro, talking to local cats, kicking litter to the kerb. I have been keeping the dog-watch, learning the texture of the night. I have been studying the madder parts of the holy book, and drawing its charts. I am ready to make it come true.

II

You hunt where you can, you with your terrorist chic, your poster of Andreas Baader, your hipster cap. You walk me round the town, gesturing: *There*, you say, *that's the station, that's the bridge.* You walk me past a postcard-pretty lake, where swans steer past boys in boats for hire; or through the market, gesturing: *here* and *here*. You are dreaming of death, among the dog walkers and the begging birds. You see blood on innocent stones, imagine your story rendered perfect on the screen.

III

They are gone into exile. Days in the jungle, nights by the sea. She spends the night hours breathing prayers: words with weight enough to slice the wind. Her son, and her son's son, gone. Her house, and her dresser, and her little dog. The wind worries past, the great sky turns slowly, the chiaroscuro of the unwired world keeps her there, watching, chin on her fist, fist on her knee.

IV

Ashes in the wind, sand between our fingers. Even the memories of memory are fading. It has been decades since this all began. All your threats have been fulfilled. The children have gone to dust, the front doors on the houses bang dully when the weather turns, and the town has been handed over to stray cats. It is time to shelve the history books, shred the archives, remove the mourning shades. Time to agree that no one has won.

On the picket line

Eggs swimming in gruel. A smear of bruised avocado. You chow down cheerfully. I slip my meal, bite by bite, to the dogs. Only the cucumber—cold, quiet, elegantly sliced—seems palatable. Shake your head at me, if you will. The world has turned sour and I can no longer hold it in my gut. *If you can't eat you can't fight*, you say, lifting a spoon to my lips. Nice try, buddy, but too late. I have already left the battlefield.

Afterword

Lately I have been paying attention to what is not being said, and to what perhaps cannot be said in everyday conversation, political discourse, or in poems. Sometimes this is a matter of secrets, sometimes of lies. But where poems are concerned, it is often the effect of the ineffable; by which I mean the attempt to name the unnameable: 'the degree to which percepts or concepts resist linguistic coding'.[i] This is a problem for poets, who so often find themselves struggling to code the something that they need to say; and the words resist them; or perhaps the words refuse to give up their secrets; or perhaps it is the something itself that keeps its secret close.

Emily Dickinson wrote in #1263:

Tell all the truth but tell it slant—
Success in Circuit lies

In a post-truth era, truth is hard to grasp. But then, it has always been difficult, has always either slipped away just when we think we have grasped it, or else crashed up against us. Come at it slant; it's safer that way.

•

John Berryman told Phil Levine, who told Nick Flynn, who told the *Washington Square Review*: 'A poet's job is not to play fast and loose with the facts of this world'.[ii] What Flynn says he took from that is 'that the world outside of our own psychic realms has its own physics and part of our job is to try to understand that and respect that'.

In this collection I have tried to find ways to approach both the ineffable and the anodyne, both the world that is outside our psychic realms (the world of animals and plants, the world of gods and monsters) and the world that is entirely within our realm (the quotidian world, the world of everyday relationships and anxieties

---

[i] Levinson, Stephen C and Asifa Majid 2014 'Differential Ineffability and the Senses', *Mind and Language* 29.4 (September): 407–27
[ii] Gonzalez, Elisa 2015 'An Interview with Nick Flynn', *Washington Square Review* 36 (Fall)

and fears). And in each case I have struggled to say what cannot be said, as well as what is said perhaps too often; and tried to find a fragment of truth in each telling.

•

Recently I attended a symposium at Reading University in the UK, titled *Absent Presences, the Secret & the Unsayable,* which circled around these sorts of questions. Particularly it invited responses to William Empson's study on *Hamlet*[iii], in which he explores the prince's tactic —'he successfully kept a secret by displaying he had got one'—as one of the playwright's tactics to grasp and maintain his audience's attention.

No doubt Empson knows his stuff when it comes to Shakespeare, but I find a more convincing and appealing approach emerging out of recent poetic works, those that do not keep their matter too close to their chest, those that attempt to make some mark, however small, on social structures, and especially on discourses of power. And here I turn to the 52nd US poet laureate, Tracy K Smith, who says:

> The way I like to understand what poems do, and what they offer, is that they bring us very close to what we knew before we forgot it. Poems are attempting to bring into familiar language the largeness and the strangeness of being alive, of human experience ... Maybe for me a poem is always about that wholeness that we originated from.[iv]

Perhaps that is where the (real) secret lies.

[iii] Empson, William 1953 '"Hamlet" When New', *The Sewanee Review* 61.1 (Winter): 15-42

[iv] Smith, Tracy K 2015 'No Secrets: A Conversation with Casey Rocheteau', *Barnes & Noble Review* (1 April)

Acknowledgments

My thanks to all those who have contributed in various ways to the production of the poems, and then their collection into this book. Members of the Prose Poetry Project, based at the University of Canberra but scattered across the globe, provided a landing pad for nearly all the poems in this collection, and in many cases gave me feedback on how they were (or were not) working. Paul Munden graciously read the whole manuscript and provided corrections and suggestions, and I have faithfully followed his notes. Philip Gross interrupted his travel to write a blurb for the back of the book (thank you Philip). The organisers and audiences of what must be one of the most precisely named readings in the world—'That Poetry Thing That is on at Smith's Every Monday'— have permitted me to read and hence test out these and other poems. The network of poetry friends and colleagues in Australia and abroad, and my beloved family, have given me heart, confidence, friendship, wine and the other elements that are necessary to start, keep going, and reach the end.

A few of the poems have been published previously:

'After the Carnival', in *Axon: Creative Explorations,* Capsule 2, February 2018

'Blanche and Henry' were featured as part of an artist book I exhibited in *Material Poetics,* ANCA Gallery, 2016

'The Loom', in *Strange Cargo: Five Australian Poets,* edited by Paul Munden (Smith | Doorstop, Sheffield, 2017)

The 'Aeneas' sequence, and 'On the picket line', in *Not Very Quiet,* Issue 2, March 2018

'War zone', in *Not Very Quiet,* Issue 1, September 2017

Finally, my thanks to the publisher extraordinaire, Shane Strange, who not only contracted this book but showed remarkable patience with my combined tardiness and wilfulness.

2018 Editions

The Uncommon Feast **Eileen Chong**
Inlandia **KA Nelson**
Peripheral Vision **Martin Dolan**
Cavorting with Time **Jacqui Malins** and **Caren Florance**
The Love of the Sun **Matt Hetherington**
Ley Lines and the Rustling of Cedar **Niloofar Fanaiyan**
Things I've Thought to Tell You Since I Saw You Last **Penelope Layland**
Moving Targets **Jen Webb**
The Many Uses of Mint **Ravi Shankar**
Abstractions **Various**

2017 Editions

A Song, the World to Come **Miranda Lello**
Cities: Ten Poets, Ten Cities **Various**
The Bulmer Murder **Paul Munden**
Dew and Broken Glass **Penny Drysdale**
Members Only **Melinda Smith** and **Caren Florance**
the future, un-imagine **Angela Gardner** and **Caren Florance**
Proof **Maggie Shapley**
Black Tulips **Moya Pacey**
Soap **Charlotte Guest**
Isolator **Monica Carroll**
Ikaros **Paul Hetherington**
Work & Play **Owen Bullock**

all titles available from
www.recentworkpress.com

www.ingramcontent.com/pod-product-compliance
Lightning Source LLC
Chambersburg PA
CBHW032046290426
44110CB00012B/973